I0791348

WITH EFFECTIVENESS WE DEFEAT RACISM

A Companion Guide to:
From the Inalienable Rights
to the
Inalienable Challenge

By Dr. George P. Banks

Elements of the Guide

*I*S THIS RACISM?

"Son, you know this will not do. We are not going to sit at this table, at the back of the restaurant."

These words came from my mother immediately as she caught my attention with her stern facial expression. I had been cheerfully looking around the restaurant, pleased that my family was there to eat and spend some time together. My parents were proud because I had just completed my graduate degree.

We had arrived at the restaurant early in the evening. Filing through the door we were greeted by the hostess who led us to a table at the rear of the restaurant. Except for a few customers, the tables were empty. As we took our seats, I wondered for a moment about where we were located. I asked myself if my family's skin color was the reason for being seated at the back of the restaurant. Taking an "objective" view of the situation, I said to myself that we were living in Boston, Massachusetts, and that the days of severe discrimination had passed for the most part. I concluded that our placement at a table in the back was probably due to the restaurant's procedure for distributing customers between servers.

However, my mother needed to say no more to me. She was speaking from the years that she and my father had spent witnessing and battling racial injustice. Also, she was reminding me not to forget my responsibility for such matters regardless of the degrees I earned. I quickly sought out the hostess as my family followed behind. Appearing courteous but a little strained, the hostess placed us at a table near the front of the restaurant.

My experience with my family served to emphasize the depth and complexity of seeking opportunity for those who have experienced a history of discrimination and have struggled with acceptance within the life experience of our nation. Even something as apparently simple as the seating in a restaurant of my African American family takes on significance with relation to fair treatment and equality.

Addressing a perception of racism can prove challenging. Human effectiveness is the basis for achieving a resolution to the issue of racism.

The overview for this Guide is provided within The Freedom Framework.

The Framework presents a direction for fulfilling a pathway for America, from a base of democracy, for the achievement of freedom, and for the growth and prosperity for all Americans. This Framework, guides the efforts of Americans to receive their Inalienable Rights, and provides the foundation to support the freedom of all Americans. This goal is accomplished by the use of our Freedom to Think to identify and build with human effectiveness to support all Americans to emerge from within their origins and circumstances to contribute to the growth of our great nation.

From the overview of The Freedom Framework, this is a guide to support us as we address racism as an obstacle to Emergence, Growth and Prosperity for All Americans.

1. What is Racism?

The approach presented in this guide begins with thinking about racism. Racism is a term that is used to identify what appears to be a tendency for some people to form and use negative descriptions and views about people who may be from racial backgrounds that are different than their own. Also, included in racism is the belief that certain races possess distinct characteristics, abilities, or qualities that indicate inferiority or superiority to one another. In particular, racism is a term that has been used to describe a view of inferiority of African Americans.

Racism is identified as a negative influence in a variety of situations where people might relate to each other, including, in urban, suburban or rural living settings, educational contexts, the workplace, or large organizations or systems of organizations in public and private settings.

Within these circumstances, racism is seen as an influence on the activity that we pursue for the intended outcomes of our joint efforts and achievements. These views of racism appear to influence assessments, decisions and actions, related to access and participation in activities and programs. There is a strong suggestion that these views of racism can become a basis for the denial of equal opportunity for racial groups for engagement in life-long activities.

It appears that people develop racist views as they receive and review information from various sources. This information might come from direct contact with people from different backgrounds or from reports from other sources about people from different backgrounds. With this information, people can form inferences, judgments or conclusions regarding a racial group or groups. However, with the development of perceptions that arise to form views of racism, the question is what is the justification or the validity of such perceptions and their influence on judgments or decisions under consideration? As people receive, review and assess the information, the question is, what are the tangible reference points for reviewing and assessing criteria for seeing other people? They might be left to make interpretations with no tangible basis to support those views.

2. The Challenge of Racism

Racism presents difficulties with identifying and resolving it. Acknowledging the persistence of racism, the dilemma is further extended by the very nature of racism. First, racism involves actions that lead to the tangible effects such as, for example, the denial of equal rights and opportunities for African Americans and others. Second, racism contains an intangible characteristic that is reflected in the interpretation of the effects, the motives or the intent of underlying actions of people that yield tangible results suggesting unfair treatment. Along with its permanency, this mix of tangibles and intangibles constitute the difficulty in dealing with racism.

Thinking about my family's experience of seating in a restaurant for service, there is a struggle with both intangible and tangible aspects of racism. Was the seating circumstance for my family created by some underlying racism on the part of the restaurant reflected in a pattern of practice of customer seating or was the seating just simply a decision on the part of a restaurant employee? Was my mother overreacting to the situation or was she reacting to a subtle form of racism reflected in a restaurant customer-seating pattern?

This restaurant experience reflects the difficult nature of racism. Given the extent of the experience of racism for my mother and her family and friends, she had a basis of concern. The types of questions illustrated in my family's restaurant experience, is a sample of the challenge of facing racism.

The difficult nature of racism is represented by a perceived image of the Beast. With eyes that exude anger and evil intent, the Beast spews flames that scorch and damage anything in its way. Likewise, racism has been described as driven by an evil intent that spews it powers to damage opportunities and lives of African Americans and countless others from different racial groups.

However, the Beast is also seen as mythical in nature. It is believed that the creature has no physical presence for it exists only in the minds or words that are indulged in the fantasies of storytelling. Indeed, racism is often seen as

mythical in nature with the identified damaging circumstances for African Americans and others accounted for only by factors other than that of evil intent. Such is the nature of the Beast of Racism.

Nonetheless, the presence of racism remains an issue in our society. It is perceived to exist in many instances. Significant among them are the disparities for black and white America in areas such as, employment, education, services received and overall quality of life. The issue is the extent to which discrimination or racism, on the part of individuals, groups, or institutions, and systems account for these disparities.

There are varying views of this issue. One is that the accumulation of the past effects of slavery and a history of unfair treatment of African Americans, account for these disparities. Coupled with this view is the belief that these discrepancies are due to underlying racism that persists to this day with a choice on the part of our society not to acknowledge this racism.

Another view is that a complex mix of factors such as income level, education, or family and community structure, account for these differences. A further view is that these disparities are only a reflection of the lack of success for African Americans in dealing with circumstances that other groups in our country have been successful in overcoming.

It is the Beast-like qualities of discrimination that makes it difficult to resolve the various views of the issue of racism. Clearly African Americans have made tremendous progress in achieving their Inalienable Rights. There are extraordinary opportunities available for African Americans and indeed all Americans. However, it may be that the Beast of Racism has only been driven under cover by emancipation, legal action, law, as well as an increased awareness, sensitivity, and political correctness that have permeated modes of public communication in our society. While in hiding, given the strength and deep-seated roots of its poison, the Beast adapts to its changing circumstances to provide for its long-term survival. The Beast thrives on confusion created by the difficulty in establishing the underlying motives or intent that lead to the Beast's scorching effects on African Americans.

It has to be said that whatever the view of the issue of discrimination, the Beast exists with its scorching effects and mythical qualities. The Beast has existed and persists to this very day. It is a deep-seated affliction that has not only had scorching effects on African Americans the intended target, but it has scorched profoundly those who have wittingly and unwittingly energized the Beast. The Beast has scorched the American Psyche and the true promise of America. It is a serious matter as to whether America can ever free itself of its racism. The question that remains is how do we address the persistence of the Beast?

3. Effectiveness and Racism

We can not eliminate racism. We can not directly address racism. Racism is the Beast. It has a presence that is both mythical in perception while also serving as the source of clearly tangible and damaging effects. It is difficult to deal with. We must recognize the circumstances that provide the opportunity for the Beast of racism.

We need to understand the relationship between levels of human effectiveness on the one hand and the presence of problems or issues of racism, on the other hand. In circumstances of ineffectiveness or low levels of human effectiveness, there is a void or vacuum created by a lack of human effort for people to work individually and together to achieve intended goals and outcomes. This void serves as "empty space" that more likely becomes filled with subjectivity related to the work to be done as well as racism and other factors such as, for example, bias, and discrimination. Ineffectiveness is a haven for racism. With low levels of human effectiveness, the Beast of Racism can grow.

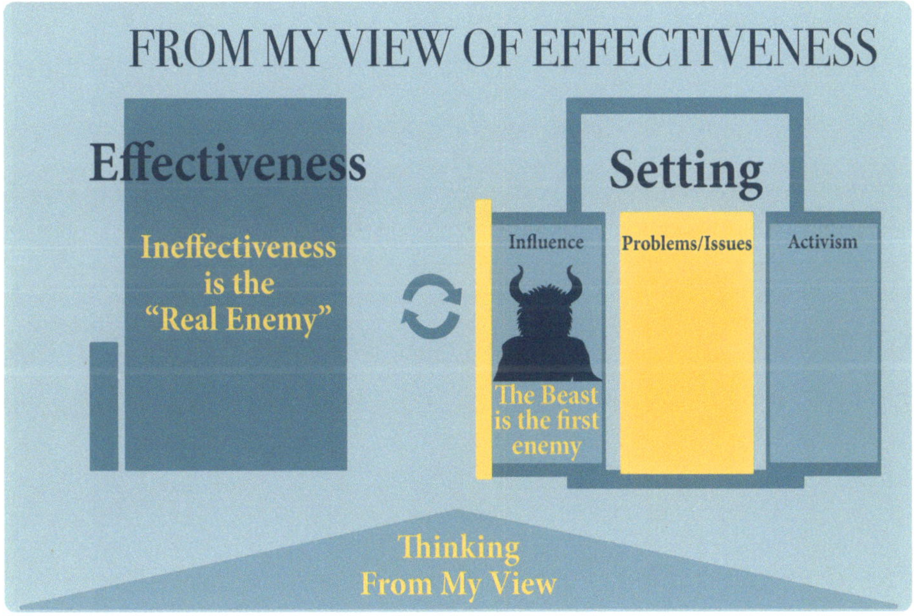

However, at high levels of human effectiveness, there is a high level of human effort for people to work individually and together to achieve intended goals and outcomes. There is little "empty space" for subjectivity related to the work to be done as well as racism and other factors such as, for example, bias, and discrimination. With high levels of human effectiveness and little "empty space," the Beast of Racism shrinks.

With the influence of the level of human effectiveness present, these interactions might serve as the overriding basis established for any and all people to have access to an opportunity. These interactions can fill in as the terms of access to opportunities for people, with relation to social relations, living, education, employment and overall acceptance in the community and society overall.

Also, with the influence of the high level of human effectiveness present, these interactions might be a part of interfacing for people at an individual, small group, large group, or organization levels or system contexts or systemic relations (that which binds people together in structured relationships for the achievement of intended tasks and outcomes) to achieve intended outcomes.

4. What is Effectiveness

I learned a lesson about effectiveness many years ago. As a Black youth in Boston, Massachusetts, riding the city bus to the Boston Latin School, the oldest public school in our country, I viewed an image of effectiveness on a poster on the inside wall above the window of the bus. As a young black male stood at the side of three young white males, one white male said to another white male, "So what, he can pitch."

Human effectiveness is the human capacity including thoughts, decisions and actions, to do something successfully or efficiently to achieve intended outcomes or results. Human effectiveness may involve the effort of an individual. Also, it may involve the efforts of individuals working together in a range of human configurations such as individuals, small groups, large groups, organizations, or systemically (systems of organizations) including organizational leadership, administration and policy developers.

Within these arrangements, individuals look to expand their individual capacities as well as work with others for the achievement of overall intended outcomes or results. For human effectiveness, an individual sees the importance of the knowledge, skill, behavior, and related actions to perform tasks and work leading to a desired result.

However, the absence of knowing how to do what is required to complete tasks for human and/or technical outcomes, is a basis for human ineffectiveness. This circumstance may be due to the lack of specification for the implementation of steps, knowledge, skills, procedures, programs or other means for work completion. Lack of this specification leaves a void or empty space with regard to the actions necessary to perform or complete work.

In addition, with the activity of human beings performing work in various circumstances, definitions and descriptions of human effectiveness for work, are often assumed or taken for granted, thereby increasing the lack of clarity regarding the work required, thereby increasing the probability of the presence of human ineffectiveness. For this reason, we often may fail to give important consideration to the element of human ineffectiveness in the performance of work. In those circumstances, where the level of human effectiveness might not be clear, issues of fair treatment in work opportunities have more of a chance to appear. Concerns about racism or other issues of subjectivity, are more likely to arise when the circumstances of human ineffectiveness may be present.

5. With Effectiveness We Defeat Racism

The challenge of racism is where to begin to address it. Racism, as perceived as existing within others, includes inferences or judgments that people make of other people. However, it is difficult to identify tangible elements of these racist inferences or judgments that people have for others. With racism, there are assumed, inferred, tangible effects on other people. It is difficult or rare to have the opportunity, to identify a tangible link between inferences, judgments or thoughts from a source of racism in a person or people, on the one hand, and actions or behaviors that can be identified as tangible effects of racism by people toward another group.

There is a challenge in addressing the specific nature of racism, prejudice, discrimination, or antagonism directed against a person or people on the basis of their membership in a particular racial or ethnic group, typically one that is a minority or marginalized.

In line with The Freedom Framework, African-Americans and others with rights denied can use their Freedom to Think to resolve problems and issues. By taking the initiative, they can first examine underlying assumptions about levels of effectiveness. Based upon that examination, they have a foundation for challenging underlying ineffectiveness, which is related to the problems or issues they seek to resolve.

Let me give you an example from my personal experience regarding resolving problems or issues from examining assumptions about underlying ineffectiveness. At one point, I was working for an organization and my supervisor at this organization, told me I was being let go from my job. Well man, let me tell you, I was upset. Being the only Black in the office, being new to the office, I began to say, "All right here it is, discrimination, racism, new to the job, for Blacks, 'last hired, first fired.'" I was angry. Then as I collected my self and as I began to think about what was going on I said to myself, "Wait a minute." I said, "What were the criteria upon which the decision to release me was based?" So I am starting to raise issues about effectiveness because in asking about those criteria I am saying, "Lack of identified criteria is evidence of low levels of effectiveness or if you will, ineffective decision-making."

So based on that consideration, I asked my supervisor for the criteria upon which the decision to release me was based. Also, I asked myself, "What were the specific definitions of those criteria?" And getting possibly, specific definitions to my question, I was ready to ask, "Ok, what is the criterion-based validation data establishing the accuracy for each of those criteria?"

So I had back-up questions in case my supervisor came back to me with criteria. My supervisor did not come back to me with criteria. So therefore, I continued asking my questions about the criteria up to the organization's executive and policy levels.

Time passed by. I received no answer to my question about criteria from anywhere in the organization. Having received no answer to my question, I took my question about criteria to the local anti-discrimination organization.

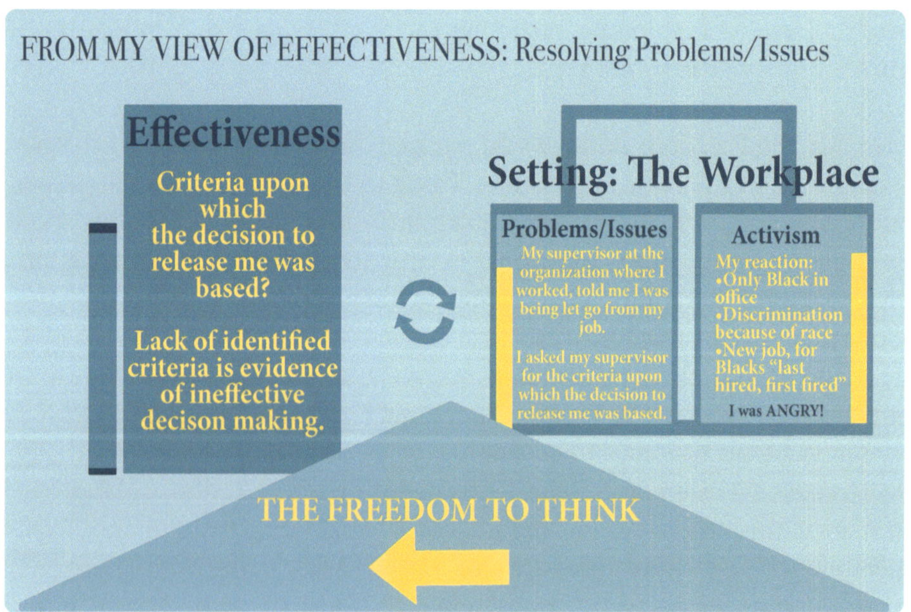

Within three weeks, I received a U.S. Postal Service certified letter from my organization inviting me to consider an offer to have my job back. I never made a complaint of racial discrimination or of racism. I only asked a question related to underlying ineffectiveness that I identified. I used my Freedom to Think to challenge this underlying level of ineffectiveness reflected in the organization's approach to decision-making. I beat the "Beast of Racism," the force that found a haven or a hiding place at low levels of human effectiveness in that organization.

I have learned that with the relationship between racism and ineffectiveness, I have an approach for addressing circumstances where racism is suspected. There is an inverse relationship between levels of effectiveness on the one hand and the presence of racism on the other hand. Racism "defeats" human ineffectiveness. With human ineffectiveness, there is a void within which racism has the room and opportunity to grow and gain strength. In this void, the growth of racism is strengthened through the presence of other factors such as bias and prejudice.

However, I have also learned that with human effectiveness, there is little space within which racism has the room and opportunity to grow and gain strength. In this "shrinking" void, racism is weakened along with other factors such as, for example, bias and prejudice.

As we increase human capacity for the knowledge, skill and behavior for performing tasks and work with others, we decrease the existence of a void within which entities such as racism, bias, judgment, racism and sexism can grow. With ineffectiveness, to varying degrees, everyone is affected. With effectiveness, to varying degrees, everyone is supported.

6. Addressing Racism: A Basic Strategy

As I review my experience in addressing racism with regard to the decision to release me from my job, I can identify a strategy for analyzing the circumstances in question with relation to levels of human ineffectiveness that might be a basis for the presence of racism in any setting of concern. The following are the series of steps that can be used as a strategy for examining a concern regarding the possible presence of racism in a particular setting or a collection of settings.

To build the strategy, start by identifying the possible context for which the issue of racism is of concern. Apply the following steps to begin the use of the strategy.

Steps:
1. Identify the setting or context where there is an issue of racism.
- Housing
- Neighborhood
- Community
- Employment
- Workplace
- Agency
- Government
- Business
- Banking and finance
- Education
- Organization
- "Systemic" - an integrated arrangement of organizations. ("Systemic Racism": the presence of racism in our lives across institutions and society overall.)

2. Identify the personnel level within the setting where there is an issue of racism. This might include:

- Customer/ service recipient
- Staff personnel
- Supervisor
- Manager
- Executive
- Policy

3. Within the setting, identify the organizational configuration where there is an issue of racism. This approach can be used at any of the following levels individually or in combination with each other:
- individuals
- small groups
- large groups
- organizations
- systemic: consisting of an integrated arrangement of organizations

4. For the level within the identified setting or context, determine the location for the decision point for organizational activity that is the possible basis for the concern for which the issue of racism might be raised. For example, the decision point might be with relation to employment in an organization or acceptance to and participation in an educational program or activity.

5. Within the identified setting or context, identify the supervising authority for the location of the decision point for which there is an issue of racism.

6. Identify and share with the supervising authority, the decision for which you are seeking information as to the nature of administrative practices. Do not bring forth an issue of racism.

7. For the key decision, ask for descriptions and any decision tools that organize the basis of the decision for the supervising authority.

8. From the descriptions and decision tools, ask for the decision criteria with which the supervising authority decision is made.

9. Ask for the specific, operational definitions of each of the criteria upon which the decision is based and ask for sample assessments related to the key decision making criteria.

10. For each decision criterion, ask for the specific research data establishing the predictive validity of each decision criterion based on a statistical correlation or predictive accuracy, with criteria external to or beyond the initial context and indicative of high levels of intended results for desired outcomes, for example, job performance related to organizational intended outcomes.

11. Upon receipt of the requested information, review the information with regard to items identified above. Note the information that was not provided or that is incomplete or unclear.

12. Provide a follow-up request for information from the supervising authority in order to have complete and clear information as requested, regarding the decision making process under review.

13. Upon receipt of the additional requested information, review it for its completeness with relation to the steps identified above.

14. For all the information received from the supervising authority, conduct a summary review of the process for the decision under inquiry and determine the completeness of the information provided.

It is important to note that a reluctance to or a failure on the part of the supervising authority, to provide the requested decision-making information, may be identified as a reflection of incomplete or ineffective decision-making or decision-making malpractice, on the part of the supervising authority. The completeness of the information provided, can be an indication of the completeness of the decision process under review that is the basis of the decision by the supervising authority that is under review.

The incompleteness of the decision process reflects possible human ineffectiveness. This suggests that such an instance of human ineffectiveness can be indicative of an opportunity for racism or other subjective factors, having an influence on the decision making-process. In addition, the incompleteness of the decision-making process that is conducted by the supervising authority, is a direct, tangible indication of the ineffectiveness of the decision-making, which makes the decision rendered by the supervising authority, an instance of decision-making malpractice. In these instances of decision-making ineffectiveness or malpractice, there is a greater likelihood of racism influencing the decision that is rendered.

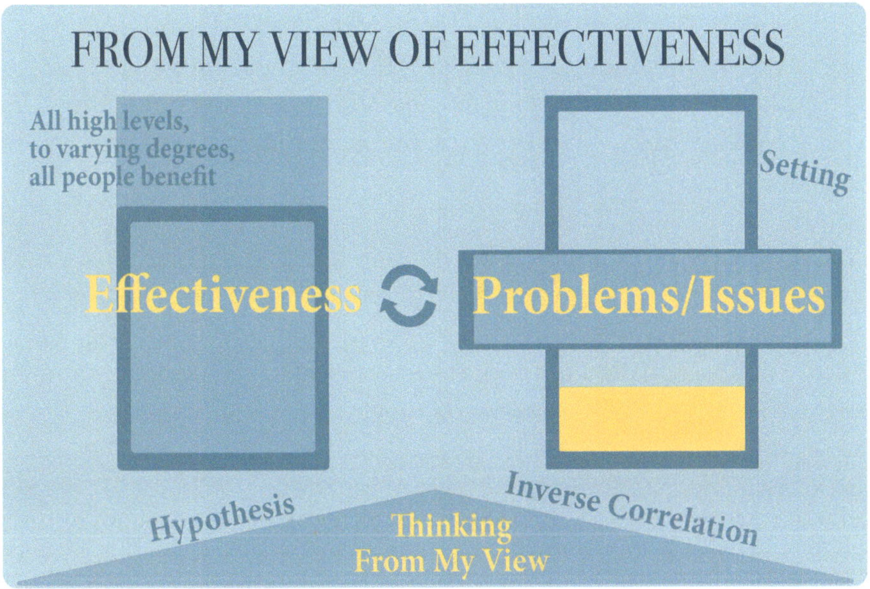

The incompleteness of the decision process under review, is certainly the basis of concern to be presented to the supervising authority. Indeed, it is a claim of human ineffectiveness or decision-making malpractice. Under the conditions of decision-making malpractice, there is a greater likelihood of racism having an influence on decisions. In a presentation to the supervising authority regarding the decision under review, the claim to be put forth is not that of racism but that there is a need to investigate the decision under review, with relation to an issue of decision-making malpractice. Additionally, this claim of decision-making malpractice, not only has implications for addressing the possible presence of racism in the decision process, but also, to varying degrees, a decision based on human ineffectiveness or decision-making malpractice, has an impact on decision-making for all individuals subject to the identified decision making procedure.

As a continuing follow-up to the identified instance of decision-making malpractice or ineffectiveness, request that the supervising authority, with organizational support, take action to correct the circumstances of decision-making malpractice. This action will provide a basis for addressing possible issues related to racial or diversity representation, for the organization or other contexts.

The Freedom Framework serves as a guide to use with a supervising authority to work for the resolution of the presence of decision-making malpractice or human ineffectiveness as well as to build initiatives for strengthening levels of human effectiveness for the organization. This approach is introduced in the review of The Freedom Framework at the end of this guide.

The strategy presented in this guide applies to the range of levels within a context for which there is a need for examination of decisions related to the presence of racism. The examination process can address a range of complexity of decisions at a particular level related to the possible complexity of contexts. This complexity of contexts ranges across individual, small group, organization or systems of organizations. Further, this analysis of the issue of racism can extend from the level of individuals to the full, complex of issues across organizations, or "systemic racism." The starting point involves identifying the key decisions and the supervising authorities responsible for those decisions.

Supervising authority or other leadership entities may not know how to address decision-making ineffectiveness or malpractice and the Beast of Racism. Indeed, they may well not understand how, in their leadership authority, they might contribute to the Beast of Racism directly, indirectly or unintentionally. Many leaders who are "well intended" may not know the complexity of the nature of racism or how to address it.

One major application of this approach is the area of public education in our nation. Because of its history of segregated education and related issues, there are longstanding, serious concerns for access to education for African American and other minority groups. From The Freedom Framework, there is an approach for addressing the complexity of critical decisions related to building and supporting the involvement of and contributions from all groups of people, to public education or organizational performance. This approach is presented in the paper, "A Standard for Quality Education," which is included in the reference listed at the end of this guide: "From the Inalienable Rights to the Inalienable Challenge: America's Pursuit of the Fulfillment of Freedom: A Guidebook for Leadership."

WITH THE FREEDOM FRAMEWORK, BUILDING THE EFFECTIVENESS

Approach to Racism for Freedom for All Americans

With The Freedom Framework we have an approach for using our Freedom to Think to build human effectiveness for achieving the Freedom, Growth and Prosperity for African Americans, for all Americans. With this approach we can address issues of social justice and growth for African Americans, for all Americans.

Social Justice is the idea that helps America overcome its history of inequities by enabling fair and just relations between individuals and society, as a reflection of the access to the distribution of wealth as well as to opportunities for personal activity, and social privileges for African Americans, indeed all Americans.

The strength of The Freedom Framework is that from its basis of science, it applies the freedom to think for building human effectiveness for two purposes. One purpose of the Framework is to Analyze to problem solve to address those circumstances where there are clearly identified issues in providing Freedom, Growth and Prosperity for African Americans, for all Americans. A serious example of these problems is the existence of racism used against African-Americans in our country. This guide provides a direction and strategy to address the issue of racism.

The other purpose of The Freedom Framework is to build to support the growth of America and all Americans. This involves using the freedom to think for human effectiveness, to be proactive to take the initiative with platforms and practices to provide all Americans the Freedom, Growth and Prosperity to support and build America for all Americans.

This second purpose of The Freedom Framework, provides a basis for a follow-up with supervising authorities, to address and resolve problems and issues identified in the implementation of the guide presented above. For example, through the second purpose of The Freedom Framework, the supervising authorities of entities, can take the initiative to use the Freedom to think to build with human effectiveness to support the growth of their organizations or other entities.

The first purpose of The Freedom Framework to analyze and solve problems is illustrated in the approach for this guide: "With effectiveness we defeat racism" and "We reduce the ineffectiveness that feeds racism."
An example of the second purpose of The Freedom Framework is presented in the paper, "A Standard for Quality Education," which is an approach for building public education for the growth of all Americans and America. This paper is included in the document that is the reference citation for this guide, "From the Inalienable Rights to the Inalienable Challenge: America's Pursuit of the Fulfillment of Freedom: A Guidebook for Leadership." Please see the reference at the end of this guide.

Both purposes of The Freedom Framework can be integrated in their implementation through using the Freedom to Think for human effectiveness to advance Social Justice and growth for America. A guiding perspective for building this integrated approach with The Freedom Framework, is presented in the reference listed below at the end of this guide: "From the Inalienable Rights to the Inalienable Challenge: America's Pursuit of the Fulfillment of Freedom: A Guidebook for Leadership."

In this reference, be sure to review: Chapter 7: "Unifying Ideology for Leadership."

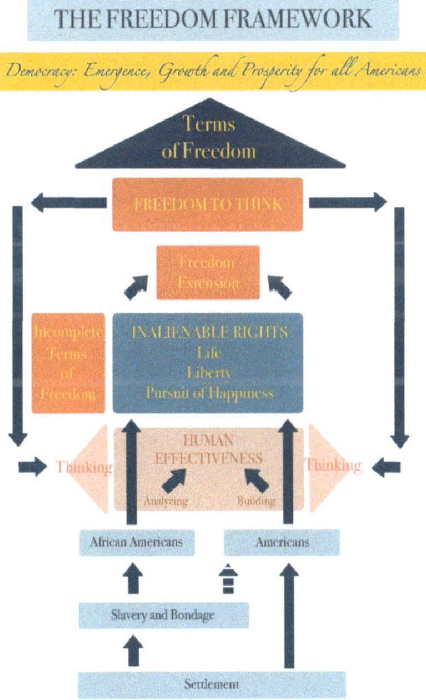

Reference for This Guide

From the *Inalienable Rights* to the *Inalienable Challenge*

America's Pursuit of the Fulfillment of Freedom

A Guidebook for Leadership

-This guidebook is for anyone who is interested in leading, no matter their experience or background. A great reader for those who are inspired by and love this country.

By Dr. George P. Banks